CELEBRATE FREEDOM

Songs, Symbols, and Sayings of the United States

Contents

PEARSON
Scott Foresman

ISBN: 0-328-03672-2

4 5 6 7 8 9 10 V055 11 10 09 08 07 06 05 04 03

Editorial Offices: Glenview, Illinois
• Parsippany, New Jersey • New York, New York
Sales Offices: Parsippany, New Jersey • Duluth, Georgia
• Glenview, Illinois • Coppell, Texas • Ontario, California
www.sfsocialstudies.com

Oh, say! can you see, by the dawn's early light,
What so proudly we hailed at the twilight's last gleaming,
Whose broad stripes and bright stars, through the perilous fight,
O'er the ramparts we watched were so gallantly streaming?
And the rockets' red glare, the bombs bursting in air,
Gave proof through the night that our flag was still there.
Oh, say, does that Star-Spangled Banner yet wave
O'er the land of the free and the home of the brave?

America

Words by Samuel Francis Smith

My country! ’tis of thee, Sweet land of liberty, Of thee I sing;
Land where my fathers died, Land of the Pilgrims’ pride,
From ev’ry mountainside Let freedom ring!

We the People

America, the Beautiful

Words by Katharine Lee Bates
Music by Samuel A. Ward

O beautiful for spacious skies,
For amber waves of grain,
For purple mountain majesties
Above the fruited plain!

America! America!
God shed His grace on thee,
And crown thy good with brotherhood
From sea to shining sea!

This Land Is Your Land

Words and Music by Woody Guthrie ©

This land is your land,
This land is my land
From California,
To the New York Island;
From the redwood forest
To the gulf stream waters;
This land was made for you and me.

As I was walking a ribbon of highway,
I saw above me an endless skyway,
I saw below me a golden valley.
This land was made for you and me.

Yankee Doodle

Words by Dr. Richard Shuckburgh

Yankee Doodle went to town,
A-riding on a pony,
Stuck a feather in his hat
And called it macaroni.

Yankee Doodle, keep it up,
Yankee Doodle dandy,
Mind the music and the step
And with the girls be handy.

You're a Grand Old Flag

Words and Music by George M. Cohan

You're a grand old flag,
You're a high flying flag;
And forever in peace may you wave;
You're the emblem of
The land I love,
The home of the free and the brave.
Ev'ry heart beats true
under red, white, and blue,
Where there's never a boast or brag;
But should auld acquaintance be forgot,
Keep your eye on the grand old flag.

1776

The first United States flag had 13 stripes and 13 stars. They stood for the 13 states our country had when it became free. Today the flag still has 13 stripes.

The United States Flag

The United States flag is a symbol of our country. It stands for the people, the land, and the freedom of the United States. The flag has changed over time.

Some nicknames for the United States flag are Old Glory, the Stars and Stripes, and the Star-Spangled Banner.

In the United States flag, the color red stands for courage, white stands for goodness, and blue stands for justice.

Did you know? *The largest United States flag is so big that it can cover three football fields. Each star is taller than a school bus.*

The flag should be raised quickly and lowered slowly. The flag should never touch the ground.

The flag should not be displayed when bad weather might damage it.

No other flag should be placed above the flag of the United States of America.

Showing Respect for the Flag

When you say the Pledge of Allegiance, stand, face the flag, and place your right hand over your heart. When you sing or hear the "Star-Spangled Banner," stand at attention. When the flag passes in a parade, stand and put your right hand over your heart.

Displaying the Flag

Usually, the flag should be displayed only from sunrise to sunset. The flag may be displayed after dark if a bright light is shining on it.

National Symbols

The Bald Eagle

The bald eagle was chosen as the national bird of the United States in 1782.

Did you know? *The bald eagle is not really bald. This large, dark brown bird has white feathers on its head and tail.*

Uncle Sam

Uncle Sam stands for the government and spirit of the United States.

Uncle Sam is dressed in the colors of the United States flag.

The Liberty Bell

The Liberty Bell is a symbol of freedom in the United States. The Liberty Bell hangs in Philadelphia, Pennsylvania.

"Proclaim liberty throughout all the land unto all the inhabitants thereof."

In 1846 the Liberty Bell was rung to celebrate George Washington's birthday. A crack in the bell became so large that the bell never rang again.

The United States Motto

Our country's motto is "In God We Trust."

National Landmarks

The Statue of Liberty

The Statue of Liberty is in New York Harbor. It faces the ocean to welcome people to the United States of America.

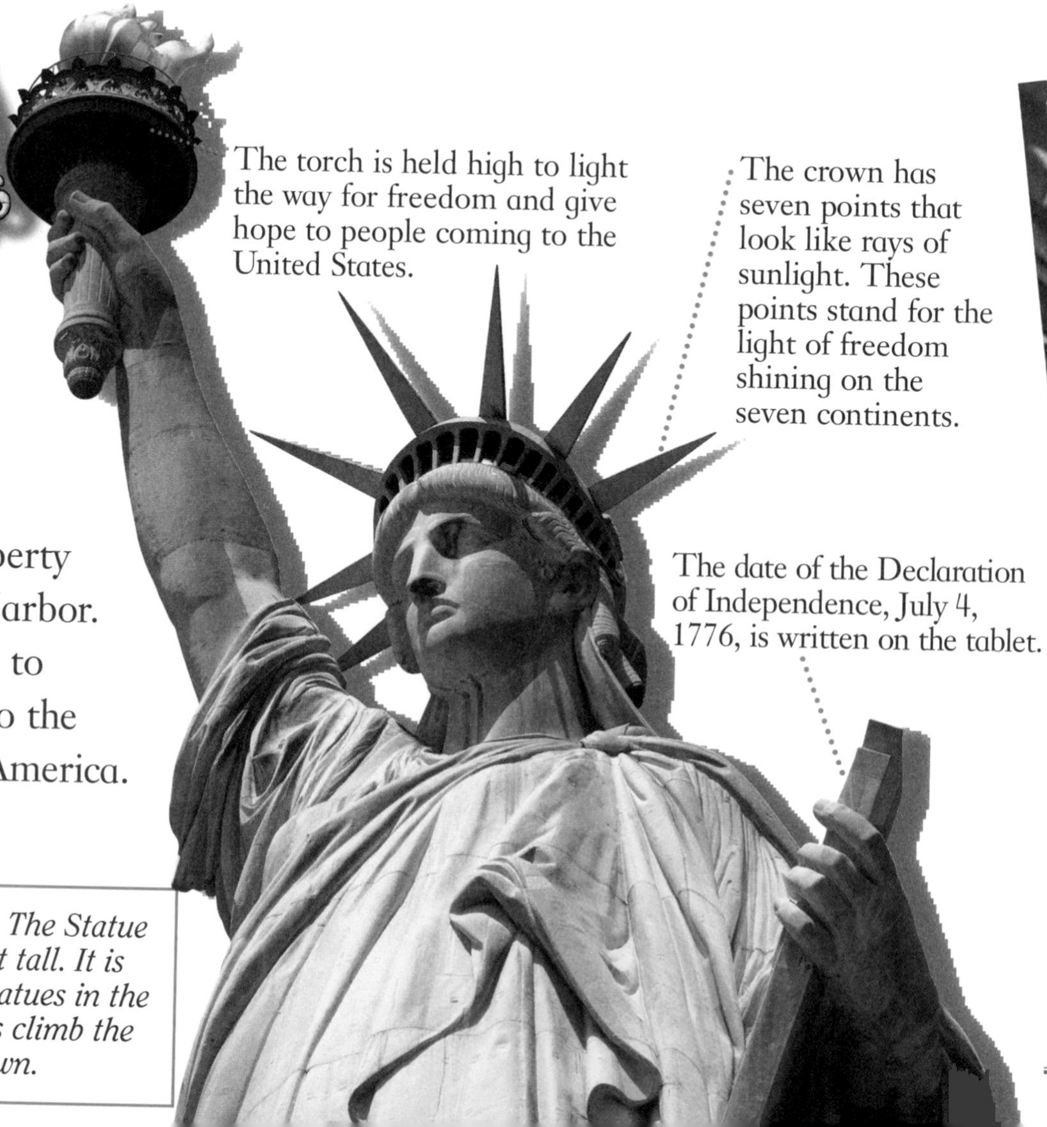

The torch is held high to light the way for freedom and give hope to people coming to the United States.

The crown has seven points that look like rays of sunlight. These points stand for the light of freedom shining on the seven continents.

The date of the Declaration of Independence, July 4, 1776, is written on the tablet.

Did you know? *The Statue of Liberty is 152 feet tall. It is one of the largest statues in the world. Many visitors climb the 354 steps to the crown.*

The words of two of Lincoln's speeches, the Second Inaugural Address and the Gettysburg Address, are carved inside the memorial.

The flags around the Washington Monument stand for each of the 50 states.

The Lincoln Memorial

The Lincoln Memorial honors Abraham Lincoln, the sixteenth President of the United States.

The Washington Monument

The Washington Monument honors George Washington. It is higher than any other building in Washington, D.C.

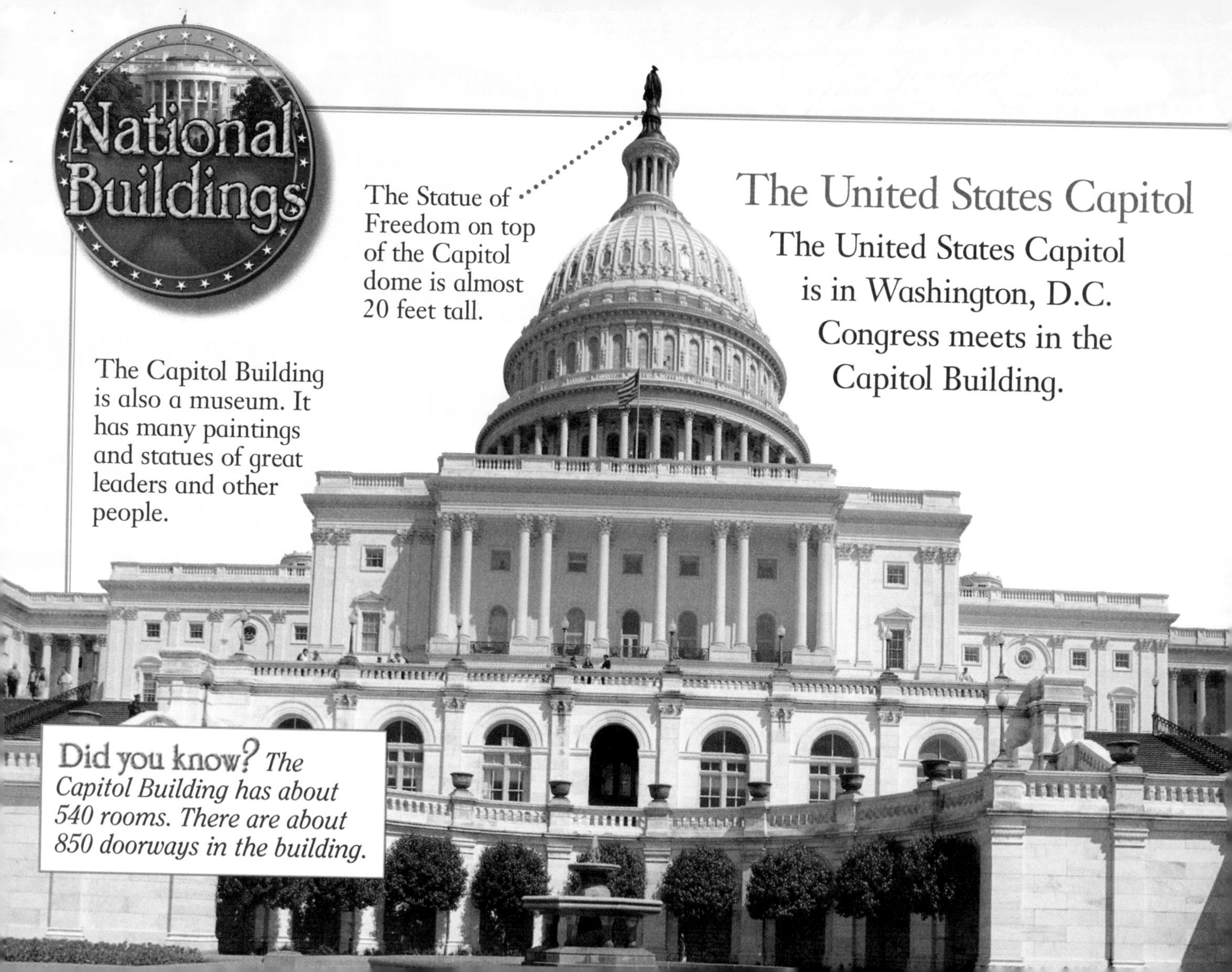

The United States Capitol

The United States Capitol is in Washington, D.C. Congress meets in the Capitol Building.

The Statue of Freedom on top of the Capitol dome is almost 20 feet tall.

The Capitol Building is also a museum. It has many paintings and statues of great leaders and other people.

Did you know? *The Capitol Building has about 540 rooms. There are about 850 doorways in the building.*

The Supreme Court Building

The Supreme Court has met in the Supreme Court Building since 1935.

The motto "Equal Justice Under Law" is carved above the main door to the building.

The White House

The White House is the home of the President of the United States. George Washington was the only President who never lived there.

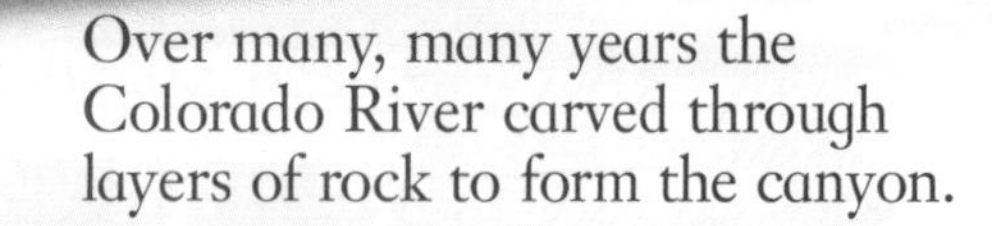

Over many, many years the Colorado River carved through layers of rock to form the canyon.

The park is home to goats, bears, moose, and many other animals.

The Grand Canyon

The Grand Canyon in Arizona is about 277 miles long and about one mile deep. In some places it is nearly 18 miles across.

Glacier National Park

More than 50 glaciers, or large masses of ice, can be found in Glacier National Park, Montana. The park is known for its beautiful mountains.

Some of the prairie grasses grow as tall as ten feet.

Some cypress trees are almost 700 years old.

Tallgrass Prairie Preserve

More than 40 different kinds of prairie grasses grow in the Tallgrass Prairie Preserve in Kansas.

Big Cypress National Preserve

The Big Cypress Swamp is home to many different plants and animals. Florida panthers, alligators, otters, and many kinds of birds live there.

The Pledge of Allegiance

"I pledge allegiance to the flag
of the United States of America,
and to the Republic for which it stands,
one nation under God, indivisible, with
liberty and justice for all."

Words of Freedom

"We hold these truths to be self-evident, that all men are created equal, that they are endowed by their Creator with certain unalienable rights, that among these are Life, Liberty, and the pursuit of Happiness."

Declaration of Independence

"We the People of the United States, in Order to form a more perfect Union, establish Justice, insure domestic Tranquility, provide for the common defense, promote the general Welfare, and secure the Blessings of Liberty to ourselves and our Posterity, do ordain and establish this Constitution for the United States of America."

Preamble to the Constitution

"... government of the people,
by the people, for the people,
shall not perish from the earth."

Abraham Lincoln

"Give me your tired, your
poor, your huddled masses
yearning to breathe free,
The wretched refuse of
your teeming shore.
Send these, the homeless,
tempest-tossed to me.
I lift my lamp beside the golden door."

Emma Lazarus

"The world must be made
safe for democracy."

Woodrow Wilson

"I have a dream that my four children
will one day live in a nation where they
will not be judged by the color of
their skin but by the content
of their character."

Dr. Martin Luther King, Jr.

"It is certainly true that a popular
government cannot flourish without
virtue in the people."

Richard Henry Lee, Signer of the Declaration of Independence

"... the most important thing in any relationship is not what you get but what you give."

Eleanor Roosevelt

"I believe ... that every human mind feels pleasure in doing good to another."

Thomas Jefferson

"If you find it in your heart to care for somebody else, you will have succeeded."

Dr. Maya Angelou, Poet

"Those who are happiest are those who do the most for others."

Booker T. Washington

"With malice toward none; with charity for all ..."

Abraham Lincoln

"No act of kindness, no matter how small, is ever wasted."

Aesop

"Never lose a chance of saying a kind word."

William Makepeace Thackeray, Writer

"The majority of the American people still believe that every single individual in this country is entitled to just as much respect, just as much dignity, as every other individual."

Barbara Jordan, United States Congresswoman, 1973–1979

"And it is the responsibility of all citizens in all sections of this country to respect the rights of others . . ."

John F. Kennedy

"We must each respect others even as we respect ourselves."

U Thant, Secretary-General of the United Nations, 1961–1971

"I am eager to learn from others. My father believed you could learn from...a farm worker or a president...and you should respect both equally."

Dr. Blandina Cardenas, Educator

". . . people might say this about our Nation: That we ensured respect for the law, and equal treatment under the law, for the weak and the powerful, for the rich and the poor . . ."

James Earl (Jimmy) Carter

Responsibility

"I long to accomplish some great and noble task, but it is my chief duty to accomplish small tasks as if they were great and noble."

Helen Keller

"And so my fellow Americans: ask not what your country can do for you—ask what you can do for your country."

John F. Kennedy

"We must use our lives to make the world a better place . . ."

Dolores Huerta, Labor Leader

"Make your life count—and the world will be a better place because you tried."

Ellison Onizuka, Astronaut

"Do the best you can in every task, no matter how unimportant it may seem at the time."

Sandra Day O'Connor

"Whatever your life's work, do it well."

Dr. Martin Luther King, Jr.

"America at its best is a place where personal responsibility is valued and expected."

George W. Bush

"I would like to be known as a person who is concerned about freedom and equality and justice and prosperity for all people."

Rosa Parks

"Freedom and the dignity of the individual have been more available and assured here than in any other place on earth."

Ronald Reagan

"Four score and seven years ago our fathers brought forth on this continent a new nation, conceived in Liberty and dedicated to the proposition that all men are created equal."

Abraham Lincoln

"The Constitution of the United States knows no distinction between citizens on account of color."

Frederick Douglass

". . . without equality there can be no democracy."

Eleanor Roosevelt

"There can be no truer principle than this—that every individual in the community at large has an equal right to the protection of government."

Alexander Hamilton

Honesty

"Honesty is the first chapter in the book of wisdom."

Thomas Jefferson

"It does not require many words to speak the truth."

Chief Joseph, Nez Percé Leader

"Give truth, and your gift will be paid in kind."

Madeline Bridges, Poet

"You never find yourself until you speak the truth."

Pearl Bailey, Entertainer and Writer

"The life of the nation is secure only while the nation is honest, truthful, and virtuous."

Frederick Douglass

"I hope I shall always possess firmness and virtue enough to maintain what I consider the most enviable of all titles, the character of an honest man."

George Washington

"There is nothing so powerful as truth."

Daniel Webster

Courage

“Only you put limitations on yourself about what you can achieve—don’t be afraid to reach for the stars.”

Dr. Ellen Ochoa, Astronaut

“The time is always right to do right.”

Dr. Martin Luther King, Jr.

“Courage is the first of human qualities because it is the quality which guarantees all others.”

Winston Churchill

“Standing for right when it is unpopular is a true test of moral character.”

Margaret Chase Smith, United States Congresswoman, 1940–1972

“Without courage, we cannot practice any other virtue with consistency. We can’t be kind, true, merciful, generous, or honest.”

Dr. Maya Angelou, Poet

“It takes as much courage to have tried and failed as it does to have tried and succeeded.”

Anne Morrow Lindbergh, Writer

Credits

Illustrations

2,3 Marc Scott; 4,5 Robert Gunn; 6,7 Tom Foty; 8,9 Anthony Carnabuci; 10,11 Cheryl Kirk Noll; 22,23 Holly Flagg

Songs

THIS LAND IS YOUR LAND, Words and Music by Woody Guthrie. TRO — © Copyright 1956 (Renewed) 1958 (Renewed) 1970 (Renewed) Ludlow Music, Inc., New York, NY. Used by Permission.
"Yankee Doodle," Words by Dr. Richard Shuckburgh from THE MUSIC CONNECTION, Gr. 2 by Jane Beethoven et al., p. 199. Copyright © 2000 by Silver Burdett Ginn Inc. Reprinted by permission of Pearson Education, Inc.

Photographs

Every effort has been made to secure permission and provide appropriate credit for photographic material. The publisher deeply regrets any omission and pledges to correct errors called to its attention in subsequent editions. Unless otherwise acknowledged, all photographs are the property of Scott Foresman, a division of Pearson Education.

12 Siede Preis/PhotoDisc; 13 PhotoDisc; 14 (TC) © Grant V. Faint/Getty Images/The Image Bank, (BR) Obverse ©, (BL) W. Perry Conway/Corbis; 15 (C) © Leif Skoogfors/Corbis-Bettmann; 16 (C) © Bill Ross/Corbis; 17 (TL) © Bettmann/Corbis, (TR) James P. Blair/PhotoDisc; 18 (C)SuperStock; 19 (TL) SuperStock, (BL) Jeremy Woodhouse/PhotoDisc; 20 (TL) © Danny Lehman/Corbis, (TR) © Jon Eisberg/Getty Images/FPG; 21 (TR) Alan and Sandy Carey/PhotoDisc, (TC) © Gary Randall/Unicorn Stock Photos; 24 (B) The Granger Collection, New York; 25 (TC, TR, BR) Library of Congress, (CL) © Bettmann/Corbis; 26 (TL, TR) Library of Congress, (BL) © Mitchell Gerber/Corbis; 27 (TL) United States Senate, (TR, BC) © Bettmann/Corbis; 28 (TL) © Bettmann/Corbis, (TR) NASA, (BL) Corbis, (BC) © AFP/Corbis; 29 (TL) © Reuters NewMedia Inc./Corbis, (BR) © Archivo Iconografico, S. A./Corbis; 30 (TL, TR) Library of Congress, (BL, BR) © Bettmann/Corbis; 31 (TL) NASA, (TR) Library of Congress, (BL, BR) © Bettmann/Corbis